LEGENDS OF CHIMA™

W9-BYO-981

ULTIMATE STICKER COLLECTION

HOW TO USE THIS BOOK

Read the captions, then find
the sticker that best fits the space.
(Hint: check the sticker labels for clues!)

•

Don't forget that your stickers can
be stuck down and peeled off again.

•

There are lots of fantastic extra stickers
for creating your own scenes
throughout the book.

DK

LONDON, NEW YORK,
MELBOURNE, MUNICH, AND DELHI

Written by Julia March
Edited by Emma Grange
Designed by Anna Formanek
Cover designed by Anna Formanek

First published in the United States in 2013
by DK Publishing
375 Hudson Street,
New York, New York 10014

10 9 8 7 6 5 4 3 2 1
001–187855–May/13

Page design copyright © 2013 Dorling Kindersley Limited

A CIP catalog record for this book is available from the Library of Congress.

ISBN: 978-1-4654-0862-4

Color Reproduction in the UK by Altaimage
Printed and bound in China by L-Rex

Discover more at
www.dk.com

LEGO.com/chima

TRIBES OF CHIMA™

Chima™ is a land like no other. In this magical world, tribes of animals walk and talk like humans, and build, drive, and invent too. For 1,000 years the tribes lived in peace, but not any more. The greedy Crocodiles, Ravens, and Wolves are battling the good Lions and Eagles over CHI—a mystic life force that gives all of them their amazing powers.

MOUNT CAVORA

CHI flows down into Chima from a floating mountain called Mount Cavora. It collects in the Sacred Pool.

CHI ORBS

In the Sacred Pool, the CHI forms into Orbs, which the Lions harvest and distribute among the tribes.

©2013 LEGO

©2013 LEGO

NOBLE LIONS

The Lions are very fair. They always give each tribe exactly the same amount of CHI.

NASTY CROCS

The Crocodiles started the conflict. They picked fights with the Lions and demanded extra CHI.

©2013 LEGO

BAD WOLVES

The Wolves are allies of the Crocs. If there is extra CHI up for grabs, they want some.

BRAVE EAGLES

The Eagles have allied with the Lions. They agree that there should be equal CHI for all.

ROBBING RAVENS

The Ravens have joined the Crocs' side—but that doesn't stop them stealing the Crocs' CHI if they get the chance!

GOOD VS. EVIL

As the two sides face off with each other, Chima rings with the sounds of battle. Which side will win—good or evil?

CHI

Everything in Chima depends on CHI. Without this potent energy source the animals would lose their powers, vehicles would not start, and weapons would be useless. Only regular power-ups using CHI Orbs keep everything going. Everyone needs CHI, but it must be shared fairly or Chima will be thrown out of balance.

CHI ORB
Most Orbs of CHI glow blue. There is a golden form of CHI too, but it is very rare.

POWER-UP
Animals power-up by placing a CHI Orb into the front of a special harness on their chests.

VEHICLE POWER
The animals' vehicles rely on CHI to power them. Each has a place to plug in a CHI Orb.

GUARDING CHI
Every tribe guards its CHI very carefully. The Lions keep theirs in a fortified mini-temple.

WEAPON COLORS
Bad animals wield red CHI weapons and good animals wield blue ones.

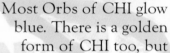

Use your extra stickers to create your own Chima scene.

LIONS

The Lions are brave, noble, and fair. They live in Lion City, a great city of stone built at the edge of the the jungle. Lions love tradition. They live by a strict set of rules called the Lion Code that they take very seriously—in fact they stick to it even if it puts them at a disadvantage. Now that's noble!

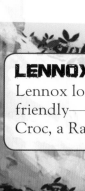

LENNOX
Lennox looks stern, but he is friendly—unless you are a Croc, a Raven, or a Wolf!

LEONIDAS
Leonidas follows orders perfectly—unless he is given more than one at a time. Then he gets all mixed up!

LAVAL
Young Prince Laval will be a great leader if he can learn to put duty before fun.

LONGTOOTH
Longtooth is the oldest Lion. He has lots of tales about his exploits, and he tells them over and over.

SPEEDOR KINGS
The Lions are fierce but fair competitors in the Chima Speedor races.

ROARING ENGINES

The Lions' vehicles are big, strong, and noisy. Just listen to those engines roar!

BRAVE PRINCE

Laval may be a youngster, but he has the courage of a Lion 10 times his age.

OLD SOLDIER

Veteran soldier Longtooth is ready for any battle, as long as his creaky back holds out.

CHI GUARDIANS

Lions have always been in charge of the Sacred Pool of CHI. That's why they are called the Guardians of the CHI.

BRAINS VS. BRAWN

Leonidas is not as strong as Crug the Croc thug, but he is a much more wily fighter.

CROCODILES

Never trust a Crocodile! Behind their toothy grins these rotten reptiles are the sneakiest of all Chima's tribes. They lurk in their squelchy swamp houses thinking up ways to get their scaly hands on somebody else's CHI, whether that means fighting, cheating, tricking, or lying.

CROOLER
Mean little Crooler loves to sneer and snipe at her big brother, Cragger.

CROMINUS
King Crominus is fiercely protective of his scaly-skinned reptile tribe.

CRAGGER
Cragger is the ambitious son of King Crominus. He lives for CHI and the thrill of victory.

CRUG
Crug is big and strong but a bit dim. He obeys all Cragger's orders—even the craziest!

CRAWLEY
Crawley is fast and wiry. His favorite move is flicking his tail at enemies to trip them up.

CROC KING
Crominus is old and wise. Unlike his son, he thinks before rushing into battle.

CROCODILE SHIPS
Crocodile ships can float on water or dive below it.

CROC SPEEDOR
The Crocodiles win many Speedor races, but they often resort to cheating.

BITTER FOES
Careful, Leonidas! Crawley is trying to grab your weapon with his magnetic reed Swampulsor.

CHI GETAWAY
Crawley must not keep his master waiting! He races back to Cragger with his stolen CHI.

©2013 LEGO

EAGLES

The Eagles are good allies of the Lions. They live in lofty clifftop houses and think lofty thoughts too. In fact, some of the other tribes say they have their heads in the clouds. The Eagles don't care. They're too busy having genius ideas and creating fantastic new technology.

ERIS
Chatty Eris spends a lot of time with the Lions, especially Laval. She has a bit of a crush on him!

EQUILA
Of all the Eagles, Equila is the fastest flier, and the fastest talker too.

EGLOR
Most of the Eagles' technology is invented by Eglor. He is the tribe's tech-head.

EWAR
Ewar really does have Eagle eyes. He's a great shot with his powerful CHI cannon.

EAGLE SPEEDOR

The Eagle Speedor always gets plenty of air as it whizzes around the Chima race arena.

BRAINY BIRD

Eglor has covered the side of Eagle Mountain with his scientific calculations.

PERFECT PLANES

The Eagles keep their battle planes, like this Interceptor, in tip-top condition.

TALKING BIRD

Fast-talking Equila is a natural for the job of announcer at the Speedor races.

FEATHERED FOES

Eagles and Ravens are both birds, but that doesn't mean they are friends.

ROUTING RIZZO

Stay away from that CHI, Rizzo, or risk a blast from Ewar's powerful cannon!

WOLVES

The Wolves live squashed up together in their armored mobile homes. They don't need personal space—the success of the pack is all they care about. Wolves don't bother with silly ideas about pride and honor, either. It they are losing a fight, they will run away. Cowards? No, just practical, say the Wolves.

WORRIZ
Sneaky Worriz is spokeswolf for his tribe. He tries hard to appear charming and nice!

WAKZ
You can tell cunning old Wakz by his bushy moustache and eyebrows.

WINZAR
Winzar has survived some tough battles—and he has the scars to prove it.

WILHURT
Fighting is all Wilhurt wants to do. He goes crazy if he can't find anyone to brawl with!

©2013 LEGO

SHREWD SOLDIER
Wakz is an experienced soldier. Like all of his pack, he is shrewd and ruthless.

©2013 LEGO

©2013 LEGO

UP FOR A FIGHT!
If the Lions catch the Wolves stealing CHI, there will be a big battle. Wilhurt is ready!

©2013 LEGO

WOLF SPEEDORZ
When it comes to Speedor racing, Wolves prefer cold efficiency over flashy moves.

FOREST FOES
The Wolves' vehicles are made to blend perfectly into their forest environment.

©2013 LEGO

TIME TO GO!
Even Wilhurt has no chance against two Eagles. Time to drop the CHI and run!

©2013 LEGO

RAVENS

The grabby, grubby Ravens will steal anything from anyone—even allies. They take their loot back to their ramshackle Nest Forts, and anyone who wants it back will have to pay for it. Ravens fight dirty, and often combine a scrap with a bit of pickpocketing. Hold on to your valuables!

RAWZOM
This clever schemer leads his Raven tribe. His name rhymes with "awesome."

RAZAR
The tribe hero is Razar. He'll wheel, deal, cheat, or steal to get what he wants.

RIZZO
Rizzo is easily the scruffiest Raven in the tribe. This makes him very, very proud!

RAZCAL
Razcal's job is to tot up his tribes' ill-gotten gains. No other Raven can count.

HOOK HAND

Razar has a hook in place of a lost talon. Some say he lost it while stealing weapons.

LIGHT FINGERED

Rizzo's Bazooklaw can be operated with one arm. It leaves the other free to pilfer.

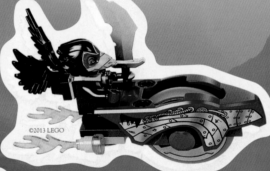

WEAPON THIEVES

Rawsom's Slashersekt is the only Raven weapon not stolen from another tribe.

RAVEN SPEEDOR

The Ravens would do anything to get their beaks ahead in a Speedor race.

RAVEN PLANES

Raven planes have beaks, wings, claws—and plenty of places to hide loot!

CHI THIEVES

The Ravens have invented a tool called a Grabberatus to help them steal CHI.

SPEEDORZ

The fastest, most exciting vehicles in Chima are the Speedorz. The animal tribes drive them in thrilling competitions at the Grand Arena. Speedorz are light and streamlined, with just one wheel—but what a wheel! Each one is carved from a TribeStone—a magical piece of Mount Cavora that fell to earth long ago.

©2013 LEGO

TRIBESTONES
TribeStone wheels draw power from nature, so they work much better in lush conditions.

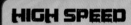
©2013 LEGO

GET SET...
The speedy one-seater Speedorz line up ready to race. Who will get the best start?

©2013 LEGO

HIGH SPEED
Speedorz can go so fast that they become airborne. Eglor flies his over a treetop obstacle.

ALL FIRED UP

Speedorz are not fireproof. Razar skillfully avoids the flames of this fiery ring.

DRIVER SKILLS

Drivers must do more than just steer. Equila takes out a row of targets as he races by.

HIT AND MISS

Winzar uses all his agility to knock over an ice tower without crashing into it.

WET WHEELS

Driving through water does not slow Leonidas's Speedor—it gives it a power boost!

ROUGH RIDE

Driving at rocks will result in dents in your Speedor, as Crominus discovers!

THE WINNER!

The Lions roar their approval as Lennox streaks home. He is the winner!

THE GRAND ARENA

Every month, Speedorz gather at the Grand Arena, with the racers hoping to win a prize for their tribe. What is the prize? A precious Orb of Golden Chi, much stronger and longer-lasting than ordinary blue CHI! Everyone waits to see what kind of course will appear. Will they have to race? Joust? Shoot targets? Dodge obstacles? Each month brings something different.

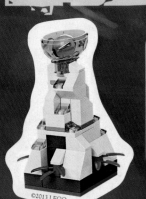

ICE TOWER
Smashing into this icy obstacle will create an avalanche of freezing shards.

WATERFALL
Riders splash through the waterfall. An Orb of CHI is well worth a soaking!

BOULDER PILE
It's quicker to crash through a pile of boulders that to go round it. Ouch!

TARGETS
Riders need a steady hand to shoot targets while driving at speed.

RING OF FIRE
It takes speed and skill to get through a fiery ring without a scorching.

JUNGLE GATES
The course ends at the Jungle Gates. Once through, riders can relax. Phew!

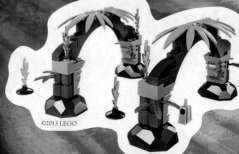

Use your extra stickers to create your own Chima scene.

LION VEHICLES

There is no mistaking who these golden battle vehicles belong to—the fangs, manes, and roaring engines tell you that it is the Lions! Lion vehicles have big grippy tracks or wheels, and simple, reliable mechanics. However, make no mistake, defeating these fast, robust trucks is a far from simple task!

©2013 LEGO

LION ATTACK
Lennox's Lion Attack has big wheels with crunching claws made of stone.

LION MISSILE
A hit from a Lion Attack missile can knock the scales off any Croc's tail!

©2013 LEGO

FIRING DISKS
When the Lion Attack opens its jaws, it is about to fire a barrage of flying disks. Quick—duck!

©2013 LEGO

©2013 LEGO

POWERED BY CHI
Liquid blue CHI flows along tubes to power the Lion Attack's fierce claws.

©2013 LEGO

LION CREW
Laval is young and fiery and Longtooth is old and wise. They make a great team!

ROYAL FIGHTER

Laval roars into battle in his Royal Fighter! He controls the CHI cannon while Longtooth drives.

©2013 LEGO

©2013 LEGO

MISSION MAP

A mission map at the back of the Fighter tells Laval exactly where the action is.

©2013 LEGO

CHI CANNON

The CHI cannon swivels on its tower. It fires rapidly, but takes a few seconds to recharge.

©2013 LEGO

JETSKIS

Lions can win on water too! They use Jetskis to raid the Crocs' ship and get their stolen CHI back.

©2013 LEGO

MANE SHIELD

The Royal Fighter has a Lion face at the front. Its big metal mane shields the vehicle from head-on attacks.

CROC CARRIERS

The Crocodiles' vehicles are all about stealth. They lurk in dark, damp places, then sneak up quietly on their foe and . . . crunch! Crude-looking and flimsy, the vehicles need frequent repairs, but make up for it by being fast, light and quiet. Rumor has it they are built using strange, slimy scales from Chima's swamps.

CROC MINI-BOATS

Cragger himself pilots this Croc mini-boat. It has two red CHI pulse guns on the front.

CRAGGER'S COMMAND SHIP

This long, low craft is ideal for hiding out in swamps. Its red "eyes" are really twin cockpits.

CROC HELICOPTER

The Croc helicopter swoops in, with Crooler at the controls. Look out, Lions!

CROC CREW
Power-loving Cragger enjoys bossing around his crew, Crominus and Crooler.

CROC MISSILE
The Command Ship's missiles are quiet, taking foes by surprise.

CLAW RIPPER
Crawley's Claw Ripper has a secret CHI compartment, giant ripping claws, and big, toothy jaws to trap foes.

CAPTURED!
Oh no! The Claw Ripper has Leonidas in its jaws. He was trying to take back the Lions' CHI.

BIG WHEELS
The big, spiked wheels of the Claw Ripper tear up anything that gets too close to the hidden CHI.

DRIVER CRAWLEY
Crawley loves the feeling of power he gets when he drives the Claw Ripper.

EAGLE PLANES

Eagles use their technological know-how to create sleek, elegant planes that are the envy of all the tribes. They are light, agile and very fast thanks to their CHI-powered jets. They are silent too, until they hit top speed. Then they emit a spine-chilling scream—the famous "Eagle shriek."

INTERCEPTOR
Eris's Interceptor has a cockpit as a head and a safe chest for CHI at the back.

COCKPIT JET
Foes get a shock when the cockpit suddenly ejects and becomes a small jet.

ON STANDBY
The body of the Interceptor stands waiting for the cockpit—and Eris—to return.

PILOT ERIS
In her Interceptor, Eris stops raids from other tribes and retrieves stolen CHI.

STRIKER POWER
The Ultra Striker has big, rugged treads. Wings hide its CHI-powered engines.

ULTRA STRIKER
Brainy Eglor has just invented the Eagles' first land vehicle. It is called the Ultra Striker.

EAGLE ROCKET
The Striker can fire two giant rockets at once. A foe might dodge one, but not both!

SURFACE TO AIR
The Striker is designed for land use, but its cockpit doubles as a mini flyer!

BRAVE EQUILA
Eagles don't like being on the ground. Equila is very brave to drive the Striker.

EWAR'S DEFENSE BLASTER
Ravens beware! Ewar's dastardly Defense Blaster has a powerful CHI cannon at the front to blast CHI-thieves from the sky.

WOLF WAGONS

The Wolves' vehicles are not the prettiest. Studded with teeth, claws, and metal rivets, they bear the scars of every battle the Wolves have fought—much to the Wolves' pride! The colors help them to blend in with most backgrounds so they can sneak up on their foes and unleash one of their trademark howling, whirling attacks.

©2013 LEGO

©2013 LEGO

CAPTURED!
Even a fast flyer like Equila cannot escape the Pack Tracker's swinging winch!

PACK TRACKER
Wakz's Pack Tracker is built for ramming. Big, toothed wheels help it to slice its way through deep forest.

WINCH
At the back of the Tracker is a winch, with a chain and two sharp claws for grabbing foes.

©2013 LEGO

©2013 LEGO

TRACKER CREW
Wakz drives the Tracker while his battlescarred buddy, Winzar, mans the cannon.

Use your extra stickers to create your own Chima scene.

RAVEN FLYERS

The Ravens' planes are so scrappy-looking because they stash their stolen loot in them! Only when the junk is hidden elsewhere can you see the uniquely unbreakable, black material that these planes are built from. Where does it come from? The Ravens are keeping their beaks shut!

CHI RAIDER
Razar's CHI Raider looks like a huge Raven. Its landing gear is shaped like giant claws.

BIG BEAK
The Raider's beak opens wide to grab CHI, weapons, or even enemy soldiers!

FLAPPING WINGS
Like most Raven planes, the CHI Raider flies by flapping its wings.

RAVEN CREW
Razar pilots the Raider, and Rizzo travels in a secret compartment at the back.

RAZCAL'S GLIDER
There is only room for one in this speedy Raven glider with its aerodynamic beak.

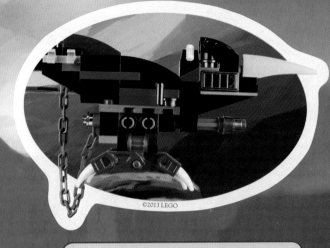

GRAPPLING HOOK
The glider has a grappling hook to pick up CHI (and any other valuable objects!)

PILFERING PILOT
Razcal swoops down in his glider to steal CHI from right under his enemies' noses.

MINI-GLIDER
Razar confuses foes in battle by buzzing around them in this zippy mini-glider.

FAST GETAWAY
After snagging a CHI Orb, Razcal soars back into the sky and away. Mission accomplished!

WEAPONS

The animals of Chima have created all kinds of weapons to help them fight off enemy tribes and protect their CHI. There are guns to blast foes off their feet, staffs to poke them out of their Speedorz, and axes to smash up their equipment. Let battle commence!

DECALUS
Lennox's favourite weapon is the Decalus. Its blade is shaped like a fierce Lion's fang.

AXCALION
The Axcalion has blades carved out of crystals from the Eagles' rocky spires.

GRANDIORUS
The Grandiorus is equipped with a row of scary spinning teeth. It's a Croc-style chainsaw!

THUNDAX
The Ravens' Thundax gives out an ear-splitting roar. No foe can stand it for long!

FLAMIOUS
Winzar uses his flaming torch to clear woods, scorch enemy vehicles . . . and cook his dinner!

Use your extra stickers to create your own Chima scene.

FRIEND OR FOE?

The Chima battles have shattered many old friendships. Even worse, they have left some animals unable to trust their allies or even some of their own tribe. Will the animals of Chima ever lay down their weapons and be friends again?

CROC SIBLINGS
Crooler is jealous of her big brother, Cragger. She mocks him spitefully when he makes mistakes.

LAVAL AND CRAGGER
As children, Laval and Cragger had fun playing pranks together. They only thing they do together now is fight.

WORRIZ AND CRAGGER
Worriz pretends to be Cragger's friend, but secretly hopes to overthrow him.

ERIS AND CROOLER
Eris and Crooler used to be friends, sharing all their secrets. Now they don't even speak!

THIEVING RAVENS
Ravens don't even trust each other. They are born thieves and go as far as stealing from other Ravens!

Worriz and Cragger

Croc
King

Mount
Cavora

Wet Wheels

©2013 LEGO

Croc Ship

©2013 LEGO

Thieving Raven

Roaring Engines

©2013 LEGO

Lion Missile

©2013 LEGO

Racing
Wheels

Talking Bird

All Fired Up

©2013 LEGO

Noble Lions

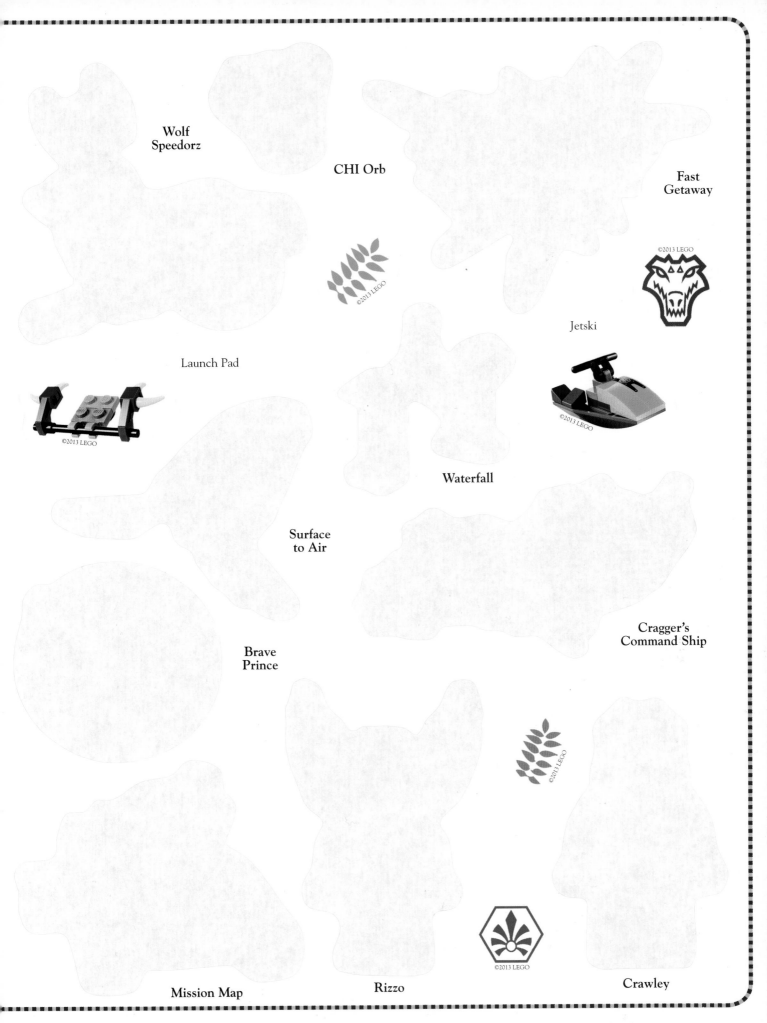

Wolf
Speedorz

CHI Orb

Fast
Getaway

Jetski

Launch Pad

Waterfall

Surface
to Air

Cragger's
Command Ship

Brave
Prince

Mission Map

Rizzo

Crawley

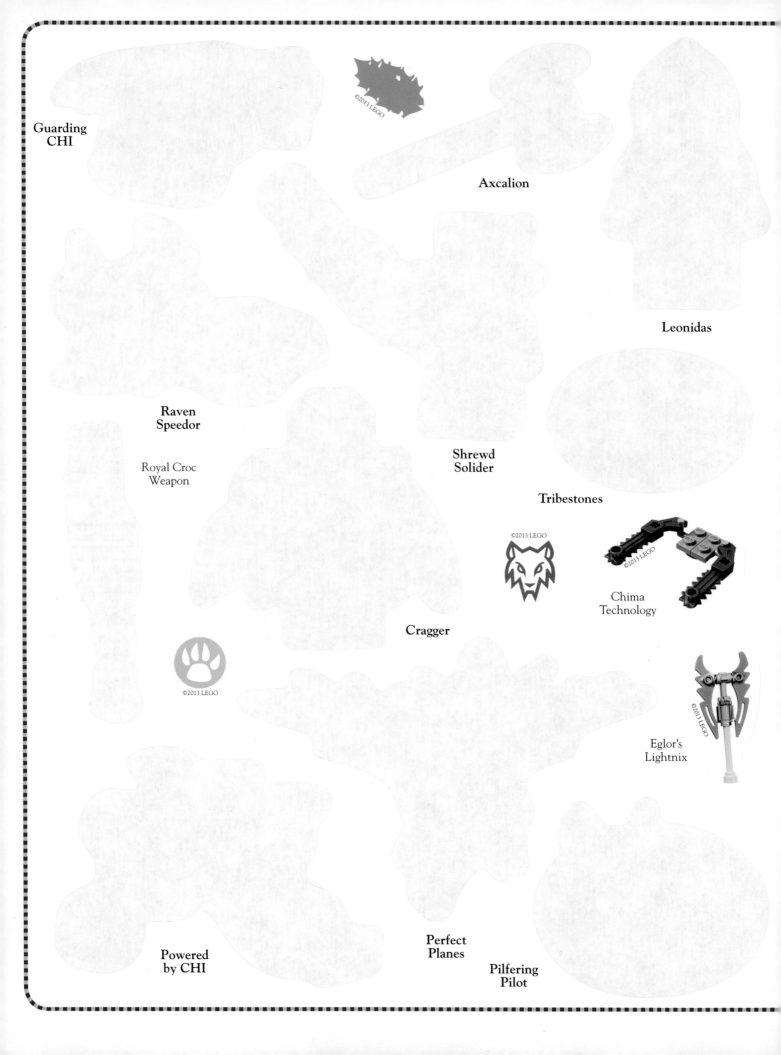

Guarding
CHI

Axcalion

Leonidas

Raven
Speedor

Royal Croc
Weapon

Shrewd
Solider

Tribestones

Chima
Technology

Cragger

Eglor's
Lightnix

Powered
by CHI

Perfect
Planes

Pilfering
Pilot

Mini-Glider

Crooler

Croc Flyer

Eagle
Speedor

Ultra
Striker

Pilot Eris

Rawsom

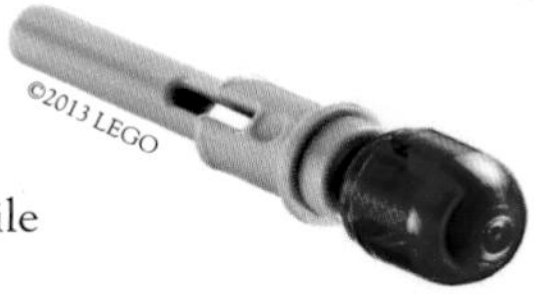

Missile

Good vs. Evil

Ice
Tower

Worriz

Eagle
Rocket

Laval

Time to Go!

Lion Attack

Jetskis

Bright
Lights

©2013 LEGO

©2013 LEGO

Rascally
Raven

Robbing
Ravens

CHI
Guardians

Firing Disks

Ever-ready
Leonidas

©2013 LEGO

Brainy
Bird

CHI
Cannon

©2013 LEGO

Croc
Attack

©2013 LEGO

©2013 LEGO

Get Set...

©2013 LEGO

Vehicle
Power

Chima
Spear

©2013 LEGO

Crocodile
Ships

©2013 LEGO

©2013 LEGO

Driver
Leonidas

Flying
Power

Striker
Power

©2013 LEGO

Decalus

Armed to
the Teeth

Ewar's Defense Blaster

Captured!

Big Beak

©2013 LEGO

CHI Thieves

One-Seater

Jabaka
Spear

©2013 LEGO

©2013 LEGO

Hit and Miss

Swamp Craft

Caught!

©2013 LEGO

©2013 LEGO

Lennox

Speedy
Leonidas

CHI
Raider

©2013 LEGO

CHI
Jahak

©2013 LEGO

Razar

Old Soldier

Razcal's
Bulwark

©2013 LEGO

Croc
Speedor

Eris and Crooler

©2013 LEGO

Rawsom's
Slashersekt

Royal
Fighter

Eglor

Eris

©2013 LEGO

Driver Crawley

Bitter Foes

Raven
Planes

Rough Ride

Nasty Crocs

Ewar

Leonidas'
Valious

Razcal's
Glider

Croc
Miniboat

Croc
Siblings

Power-Up

Speedor King

Krank

Jungle Gates

Claw Ripper

Lion Crew

Grappling
Hook

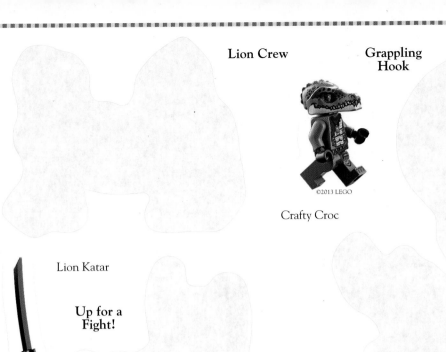

Crafty Croc

Lion Katar

Up for a
Fight!

Brave
Eagles

Fire Power

Weapon
Thieves

Driver
Skills

Winzar

Weapon
Colors

Winch

CHI
Getaway

Bad Wolves

Wakz

Routing
Rizzo

Propeller
Power

Flamious

Raider Missile

Cruel
Croc

Laval and Cragger

Longtooth

Interceptor

Croc Crew

Jetskiing
Laval

Wise Ewar

Mane Shield

Raven Crew

Equila

CHI Orbs

Thieving Ravens

Laval's Jetski

Winzar's Slizar

Interceptor Missile

CHI Jabaka

Forest Foes

Boulder Pile

Brain vs. Brawn

Open Jaws

On Standby

Ring of Fire

Wilhurst

Thundax

Light Fingered

Crug

Lennox the Lion

Flapping Wings

Hook Hand

Targets

Eglor's Jabahak

Brave Equila

Big Wheels

©2013 LEGO

Wilhurst's
Jahakastaff

©2013 LEGO

Cockpit Jet

©2013 LEGO

Lennox's
Lion Attack

©2013 LEGO

©2013 LEGO

**Pack
Tracker**

**Feathered
Foes**

Razcal

Jetski

©2013 LEGO

©2013 LEGO

Crominus

**Tracker
Crew**

The Winner!

EXTRA STICKERS

©2013 LEGO

©2013 LEGO

©2013 LEGO

EXTRA STICKERS

EXTRA STICKERS

©2013 LEGO

EXTRA STICKERS

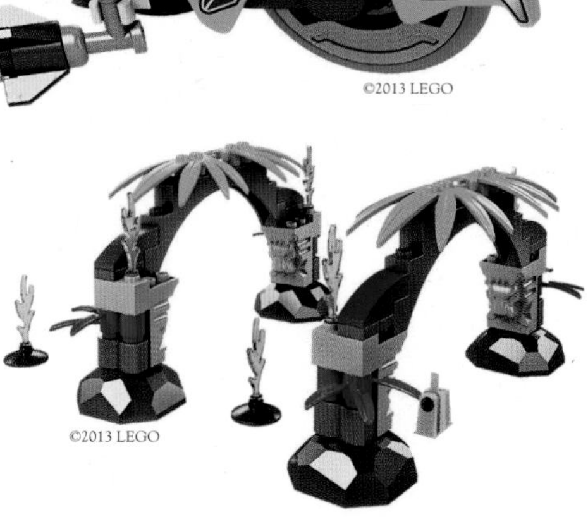

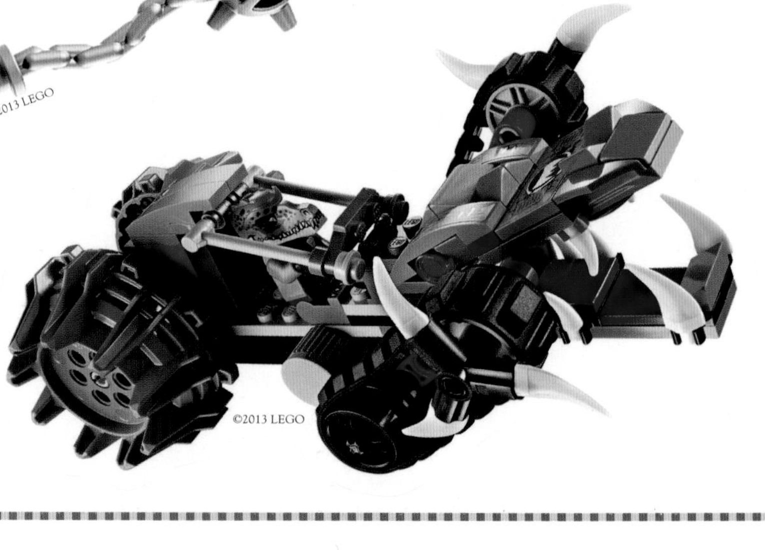

©2013 LEGO

©2013 LEGO

©2013 LEGO

©2013 LEGO

©2013 LEGO

©2013 LEGO

©2013 LEGO

©2013 LEGO

©2013 LEGO

©2013 LEGO

©2013 LEGO

©2013 LEGO

EXTRA STICKERS

©2013 LEGO

©2013 LEGO

©2013 LEGO

©2013 LEGO

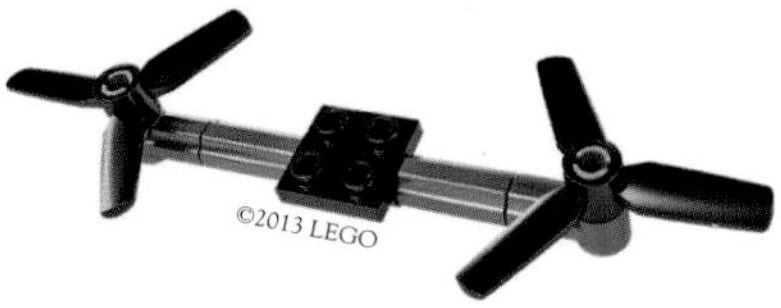

©2013 LEGO

©2013 LEGO

©2013 LEGO

©2013 LEGO

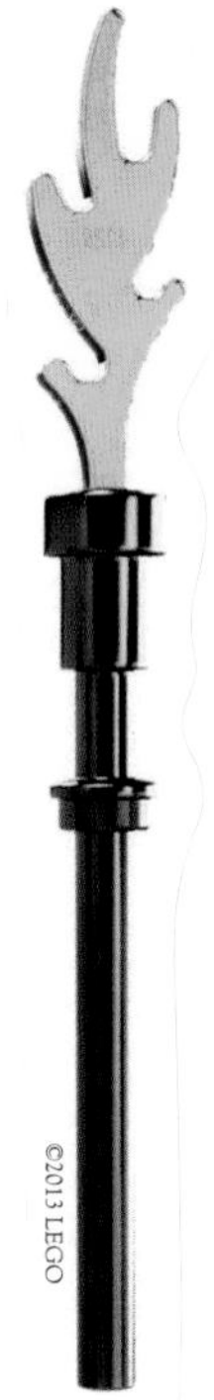

©2013 LEGO

©2013 LEGO

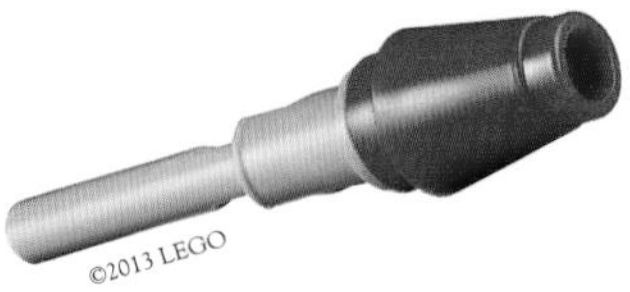

©2013 LEGO

©2013 LEGO

©2013 LEGO

©2013 LEGO

©2013 LEGO

©2013 LEGO

©2013 LEGO
©2013 LEGO
©2013 LEGO
©2013 LEGO
©2013 LEGO
©2013 LEGO
©2013 LEGO
©2013 LEGO
©2013 LEGO
©2013 LEGO
©2013 LEGO
©2013 LEGO
©2013 LEGO
©2013 LEGO
©2013 LEGO

©2013 LEGO

©2013 LEGO

©2013 LEGO

©2013 LEGO

©2013 LEGO

©2013 LEGO

©2013 LEGO

©2013 LEGO

©2013 LEGO

©2013 LEGO

©2013 LEGO

©2013 LEGO

©2013 LEGO

©2013 LEGO

©2013 LEGO

©2013 LEGO

©2013 LEGO

©2013 LEGO

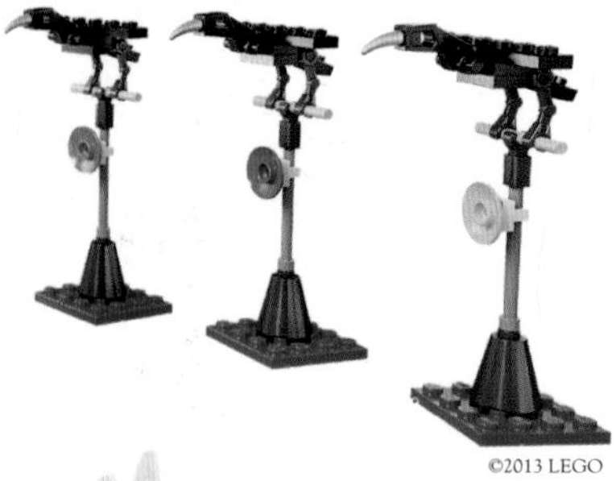

EXTRA STICKERS

©2013 LEGO

EXTRA STICKERS